MW00914868

THIS CHINGONA COLORING BOOK BELONGS TO:

>>>   <<<

CHRISTINA TAFOYA

WWW.EXPRESSLOVECOACHING.COM

ALL RIGHTS RESERVED

THIS COLORING BOOK IS
DEDICATED TO PAST,
CURRENT AND FUTURE YOUTH.
MAY YOU CONTINUE TO
COLOR THE WORLD WITH
YOUR BRAVERY AND
RESILIENCE.

I CREATED CHINGONA AFFIRMATION COLORING BOOKS TO HELP WITH GROUNDING AND THE AFFIRMATIONS TO REMIND YOU OF THE UNIQUE AND BEAUTIFUL CHINGONAS YOU ARE!

RESEARCH SUGGESTS THAT COLORING MAY LOWER YOUR STRESS, AID IN RELAXATION, BOOST YOUR CREATIVITY, AND MAY EVEN HELP IMPROVE YOUR SLEEP!

I MADE THESE COLORING BOOKS SMALLER THAN THE BIG STORE MANUFACTURED COLORING BOOKS BECAUSE I FOUND THE OTHER BOOKS WERE SO OVERWHELMING FOR ME AND I WOULD FEEL DISCOURAGED IF I DIDN'T GET TO FINISH A SHEET.

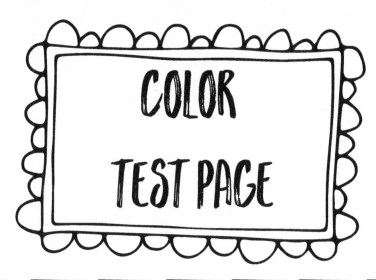

COLOR TEST PAGE

SOMOS SEMILLAS

I AM GRATEFUL FOR

- ○ _____
- ○ _____
- ○ _____
- ○ _____
- ○ _____
- ○ _____
- ○ _____
- ○ _____

CHINGONA
COMO
MI MADRE

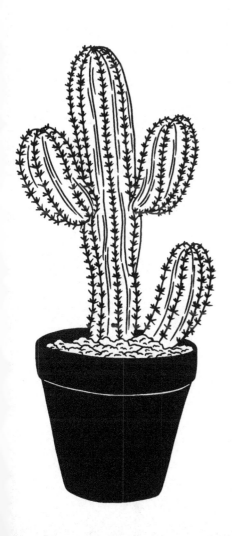

DOODLE HERE!

I AM GRATEFUL FOR

- ○ _____
- ○ _____
- ○ _____
- ○ _____
- ○ _____
- ○ _____
- ○ _____
- ○ _____

WELL BEHAVED MUJERES RARELY MAKE HISTORY

I AM GRATEFUL FOR

- ○ _____
- ○ _____
- ○ _____
- ○ _____
- ○ _____
- ○ _____
- ○ _____
- ○ _____

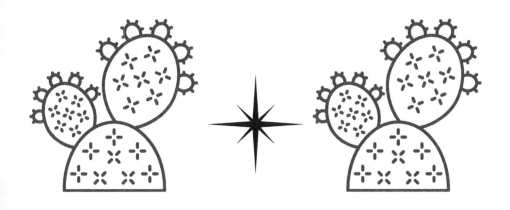

SOY

MAGIA

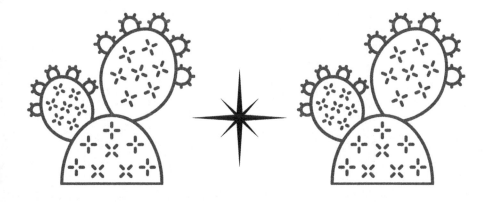

YO NO
SOY DE
NADIE

DOODLE HERE!

BEAUTIFULLY

BROWN

BADASS

CONFIO
EN MI FUERZA

_____
_____
_____
_____
_____
_____
_____
_____

I AM

WORTHY

I AM GRATEFUL FOR

○ _____

○ _____

○ _____

○ _____

○ _____

○ _____

○ _____

○ _____

I AM ENOUGH

I AM

POWERFUL y

PELIGROSA

ERES

ILIMITADA

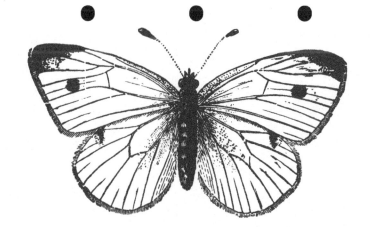

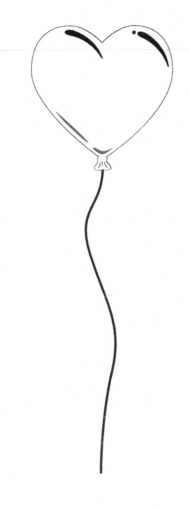

DEJALO IR

I AM GRATEFUL FOR

- ○ _____
- ○ _____
- ○ _____
- ○ _____
- ○ _____
- ○ _____
- ○ _____
- ○ _____

A LITTLE EXTRA, BUT ALWAYS WORTH IT!

ERES

CAPAZ

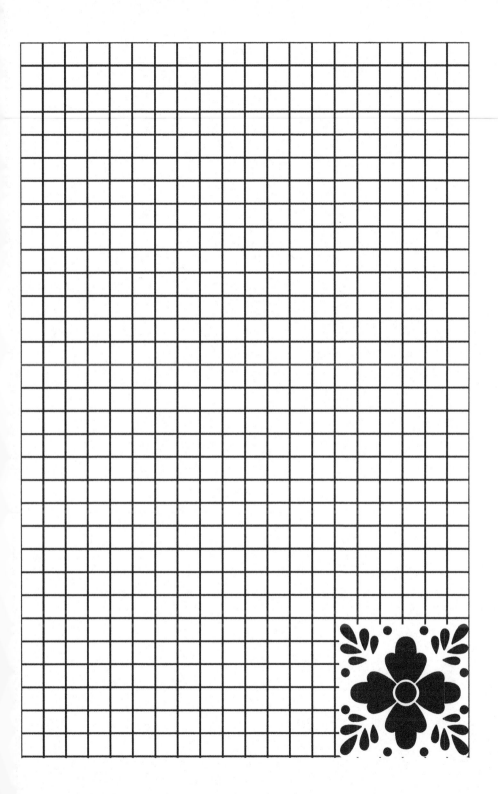

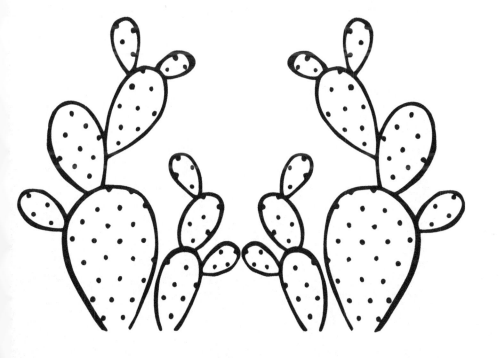

I AM GRATEFUL FOR

- ○ _____
- ○ _____
- ○ _____
- ○ _____
- ○ _____
- ○ _____
- ○ _____
- ○ _____

THE END!

PLEASE GO CHECK OUT ALL MY OTHER PRODUCTS @

WWW.EXPRESSLOVECOACHING.COM

CHRISTINA TAFOYA
ALL RIGHTS RESERVED

Made in the USA
Las Vegas, NV
15 December 2023

82938285R00056